In the woodland of wonders,

a dead tree stands tall.

You might think it is useless

and does nothing at all.

If you look a bit closer,
you'll begin to see
that although it is dead,
there is life in this tree.

In the trunk, there's a hole.
In the hole, there's a nest—
a young woodpecker's home.
Shh, they must rest.

Bugs like weevils and ants,
are incredibly small.
On the bark, take a look
as they eat the tree wall.

High above in the tree,
on clear, sunny warm days,
a young snake on a branch,
gets warm soaking up rays.

Oh, but wait, what is that snuggled up to the trunk? It's a camouflaged owl looking out for a skunk!

The dead snag of the tree
becomes this eagle's perch
and the keen hunter's eyes
focus in on the search.

Many fungi now grow
to break down the dead tree.
Their mycelium fibres
set nutrients free.

In the dirt of the Earth,
these rich nutrients belong,
where they'll help the next seedlings
to grow big and strong.

Our dead trees are important,
as now you have seen.
For so many still need them,
long after they're green.

Now with all that you've learned,

it's your turn to tell

how a tree's legacy lives

beyond its last cell.

Dedicated to
my son Beau

Inspired by my environmental science background,
and educating our little humans about our natural environment.

FIELD KITS Publishing

March 2024

Author

Kenzie Field

Editor

Kathryn Boucher & Jaimee Guenther

Illustrator

Canva AI

ISBN: 978-1-7383200-2-8

© All rights reserved. No part of this book may be reproduced in any form or by any electronic or mechanical means, including information storage and retrieval systems, without permission in writing from the publisher and copyright holder, except in the case of brief quotations embodied in critical articles and reviews. This is a work of creative nonfiction. Some parts have been fictionalized to varying degrees.

Woodland of Wonders Book Series

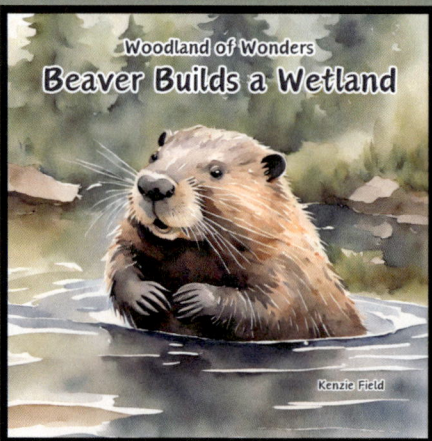

www.ingramcontent.com/pod-product-compliance
Lightning Source LLC
Chambersburg PA
CBRC091453160426
43209CB00024B/1886